To whom do you pray?

To whom do you pray?

by Leonard Layne
and Mark Best

CHAPTER TWO • FOUNTAIN HOUSE
CONDUIT MEWS • LONDON • ENGLAND

To Whom do You Pray? by Leonard Layne, Cambridge, Mass, USA and Mark Best, Blackburn, Lancs, UK

Copyright © 2006 L Layne & M Best and Chapter Two Trust, London
ISBN 1 85307 210 9
Originally published in Truth & Testimony magazine 2003

CHAPTER TWO
Fountain House, Conduit Mews, London SE18 7AP, England
www.chaptertwobooks.org.uk
e-mail chapter2uk@aol.com

Distributors:
• Bible, Book and Tract Depôt, 23 Santarosa Avenue, Ryde, NSW 2112, Australia
• The Bible House, Gateway Mall, 35 Tudor Street, Bridgetown, Barbados, WI
• Believers Bookshelf, 5205 Regional Road 81, Unit 3, Beamsville, ON, L0R 1B3, Canada
• Bible Treasury Bookstore, 46 Queen Street, Dartmouth, Nova Scotia, B2Y 1G1, Canada
• El-Ekhwa Library, 3 Anga Hanem Street, Shoubra, Cairo, Egypt
• Bibles & Publications Chrétiennes, 30 rue Châteauvert, 26000 Valence, France
• CSV, An der Schloßfabrik 30, 42499 Hückeswagen, Germany
• Christian Truth Bookroom, Paddisonpet, Tenali 522 201, Andhra Pradesh, India
• Words of Life Trust, 3 Chuim, Khar, Mumbai, 400 052, India
• Words of Truth, 38-P.D.A Lamphelpat, Imphal 795 004, Manipur, India
• Uit het Woord der Waarheid, Postbox 260, 7120AG Aalten, Netherlands
• Bible and Book Depot, Box 25119, Christchurch 5, New Zealand
• Echoes of Truth, No 11 Post Office Road, P.O. Box 2637, Mushin, Lagos, Nigeria
• Kristen Litteratur, Tjøsvoll øst, 4270 Åkrehamn, Norway
• Grace & Truth Book-room, 87 Chausee Road, Castries, St. Lucia, WI
• Chapter Two S.A., Box 2234, Alberton 1450, South Africa
• Beröa Verlag, Zellerstrasse 61, 8038 Zürich, Switzerland
• Éditions Bibles et Littérature Chrétienne, La Foge C, Case Postale,
  1816 Chailly-Montreux, Switzerland
• Chapter Two Bookshop, 199 Plumstead Common Road, London, SE18 2UJ, UK
• HoldFast Bible & Tract Depôt, 41 York Road, Tunbridge Wells, Kent, TN1 1JX, UK
• Words of Truth, PO Box 147, Belfast, BT8 4TT, Northern Ireland, UK
• Believers Bookshelf Inc., Box 261, Sunbury, PA 17801, USA

Printed in the United Kingdom by Crossprint Limited, Newport, Isle of Wight

To whom do you pray?

Introduction

The following essay aims at defending the Biblical pattern for addressing the blessed Son of God in prayer and worship. Although this pattern is denied by some denominations, it will be shown that in the New Testament prayer was not only offered to God the Father but also to the Lord Jesus Christ. Supportive evidence will also be culled from history and from hymns. Prayer is to be directed to the Father or to the Son as Lord, but there is no Scriptural authority for prayer to the Holy Spirit. He is the divine Illuminator. He brings glory to the Son (John 16:13-14) as the Son reveals the Father (John 1:18). Normally, prayer is to God the Father (see Gal. 4:6) in the name of the Lord Jesus Christ (John 14:13), but we will not deal with this here. Our theme is prayer to Christ as seen in the Gospels, the Acts, and the Epistles, and also in the history of the church and its hymns.

L Layne, Cambridge, Mass.
2006

PRAYER TO CHRIST IN THE GOSPELS

Jesus' disciples addressed Him, called upon Him and prayed to Him during His earthly pathway. Matthew, Mark, Luke and John are full of wonderful examples of the twelve and others calling upon the Lord Jesus. It is noteworthy to observe that He was never directly addressed as 'Jesus.' He was called Lord, Master or Rabbi. Notice the following examples:

1) 'And when he [Jesus] was entered into a ship, his disciples followed him. And, behold, there arose a great tempest in the sea, insomuch that the ship was covered with the waves: but he was asleep. And his disciples came to him, and awoke him, saying, Lord, save us: we perish' (Matt. 8:23-25). They recognized his ability to deliver from danger. How fitting the Old Testament statement: 'whosoever shall call on the name of the Lord shall be delivered' (Joel 2:32). This was indeed a cry for deliverance. He heard and answered their prayer. He is 'the same yesterday, and to day, and for ever' (Heb. 13:8). He can deliver us today if we call upon Him.

2) Confession of sin was made to Christ. This not only gives evidence of His deity, but demonstrates the fact that Christ was addressed. Early in the Lord's public ministry, Peter acknowledged the reality of his own sinfulness. He fell down at Jesus' knees, saying, 'Depart from me; for I am a sinful man, O Lord' (Luke 5:8).

3) On the mount of transfiguration, when the Lord was transfigured in the presence of three favoured disciples and two Old Testament saints, Moses and Elijah, Peter answered and said unto Jesus, 'Lord, it is good for us to be here ...' (Matt. 17:4). These disciples recognized that the Lord Jesus

was more than a mere man. They looked up to him as the Messiah (the Christ or Anointed of God), now appearing in a glorified state right before their very eyes. When we are conscious of the Lord's presence we too can declare our appreciation for such a privilege: 'Lord, it is good for us to be here.'

4) On another very different note, there was a man who was crucified with Jesus. We do not know much about him, other than the fact that he was a common criminal, a thief. After he and another executed man hurled insults at the Lord Jesus, he came to his senses. He said to Jesus, 'Lord, remember me when thou comest into thy kingdom.' The response is majestic: 'Verily (truly) I say unto thee, To day shalt thou be with me in paradise' (Luke 23:42-43). Again we see the fulfilment of the promise that all who call upon the name of the Lord shall be saved. What an encouragement this is, that even deathbed prayers offered in faith are heard and answered.

From these few references we can see prayers were spoken to the Lord Jesus in the gospels. He was God 'manifest in the flesh' (1 Tim. 3:16), though in lowliness here on the earth. We also observe that He not only heard those prayers but answered them.

PRAYER TO CHRIST IN THE ACTS

After the Lord Jesus Christ ascended back to the Father's right hand, He sent the Holy Spirit, the promise of the Father (Acts 2). The book of Acts is often described as the Acts of the Holy Spirit. This divine Person is seen moving, speaking and directing throughout the book. Nevertheless, there is no example of the disciples praying to Him even though He is a divine person. However, there are a number of examples of these early Christians praying to the risen and exalted Christ. Someone has referred to the name 'Lord Jesus' as His assembly name. This is because Acts portrays the interaction between the body on earth and the Head in heaven, and we find Him addressed as Lord Jesus or Lord rather than as Christ Jesus or Jesus Christ.

5) Stephen, one of the chosen servants of the assembly in Jerusalem (Acts 6:5), was the object of persecution. After a boldly delivered sermon to the Sanhedrin (or Council), he was stoned to death, becoming the first martyr of the faith (Acts 7:58-60). He called upon God in prayer saying, 'Lord Jesus, receive my spirit.' The Lord was now in heaven as Stephen demonstrated when he declared, 'Behold, I see the heavens opened, and the Son of man standing on the right hand of God' (Acts 7:56). Later, as he continued to be pelted with stones, he knelt (what a posture for prayer![1]) and cried with a loud voice, 'Lord, lay not this sin to their charge.' He fulfilled the teaching of his blessed Lord: 'pray for them which despitefully use you, and persecute you' (Matt. 5:44). Nothing has changed since the disciples' day in the book of Acts; in moments of danger or need, the Christian cries out, 'Lord Jesus.'

6) When the risen Christ addresses Saul (later called Paul), 'Saul, Saul, why persecutest thou me?', he replies in a definite

---

[1] Kneeling is the most common posture for prayer in Scripture. Standing to pray is also recorded, but only one instance of sitting (by a king – David). Reverence is important. Casual conduct in the Divine presence – praying with hands in one's pockets or slouching – is unbecoming.

prayer to the exalted Christ, 'Who art thou, Lord?' and again, 'Lord, what wilt thou have me to do?' (Acts 9:5-6 and 22:10). He prays that he might know the will of God. He is a submissive man; on his face before His sovereign. His response is not like that of Peter concerning the apostle John, 'Lord: and what shall this man [John] do?' (John 21:21). He is not occupied with God's will for others but for himself. Here is a praying man. His prayer is directed to the Lord Jesus Christ.

PRAYER TO CHRIST IN THE EPISTLES

7) Salvation, particularly justification by faith alone, is the theme of the mighty epistle of Paul to the Romans. After declaring man's ruin by sin, and sin's remedy in the gospel, the apostle sets forth the need to confess Jesus as Lord. He refers to the Old Testament verse we have already considered, 'For whosoever shall call upon the name of the Lord shall be saved' (Rom. 10:13). Since the Lord Jesus is clearly presented in the New Testament as the Jehovah of the Old, there is no difficulty praying directly to Him as well as to the Father. In fact, prayer to Him demonstrates the validity of His claim to deity.

8) Paul was afflicted with a bodily affliction later in his service for the Lord Jesus, which he referred to as 'a thorn in the flesh, the messenger of Satan' (2 Cor. 12:7). He prayed for deliverance as many had prayed for divine intervention and rescue before him. They experienced the Lord's deliverance but Paul's request was denied even though he prayed for it on three occasions. He prayed, not to God the Father, but to the Lord Jesus Christ, and writes of the experience: 'For this thing

I besought the Lord thrice, that it might depart from me' (2 Cor. 2:8). The Lord said, 'no', but added, 'my grace is sufficient for thee: for my strength is made perfect in weakness' (2 Cor. 12:9).

9) In 1 Corinthians, 'the epistle of His Lordship', where the word 'Lord' (Greek: kyrios, here meaning: sovereign master) is used some 69 times, Paul declares the assembly to consist of those who pray directly to the Lord Jesus. Notice the statement in chapter 1, verse 2: '... to the assembly of God which is in Corinth, to [those] sanctified in Christ Jesus, called saints, with *all that in every place call on the name of our Lord Jesus Christ*, both theirs and ours' (JND, N.Tr.).

The letter is addressed to the church of God, not to individual Christians, and takes in the entire visible community of believers; what he calls in another place, the household of faith (Gal. 6:10). The theme is church order, and he writes to those who disagree with him on the subject of head coverings: 'But if any one think to be contentious, we have no such custom, nor the assemblies of God' (1 Cor. 11:16 N.Tr.) One of the marks of God's assembly is this very thing: its members call upon the name of our Lord Jesus Christ. This is not simply prayer in His name, but calling upon that blessed name; that is addressing Him directly.

10) In 2 Timothy, Paul describes times of departure from the truth and failure, but writes that there will still be some who call upon the name of the Lord. He encourages Timothy: 'Flee also youthful lusts, but follow righteousness, faith, charity, peace with them that call on the Lord out of a pure heart' (2 Tim. 2:22).

In a day when the house of God (God's assembly), described in 1 Timothy as that which is genuine, is scattered throughout the 'great house' (Christendom), described in 2 Timothy as that which is false, there are those who desire to call on the Lord out of a pure heart (i.e. one with unmingled motives).

How solemn a matter it is that many do not pray to the Son of God. It is even more solemn that some try to hinder others from doing so by their teaching!

11) In the Revelation, the very last prayer in the Bible is offered to the Son of God: 'Even so, come, Lord Jesus' (Rev. 22:20). How precious it is that those who know Him call unto Him for His return so that they might know His presence in all its fullness. This demonstrates their desire to be near the object of their hearts' affection.

PRAYER TO CHRIST IN HISTORY

The following historical examples are drawn from Ambrose, a 4th century church leader; John Owen, a noted 17th century reformed theologian; and John Nelson Darby, a prolific writer among the 'Plymouth Brethren' in the 19th century. These writers demonstrate the Biblical pattern of prayer and worship to God the Son. This will clearly show that prayer has been offered to the Lord Jesus at all stages of the church's history.

a) The Te Deum of Ambrose, 4th century

> O Christ, thou art the King of glory!
> Thou art the everlasting Son of the Father.

When Thou tookest upon Thee to deliver man,
Thou didst not disdain the Virgin's womb.
Having overcome the sting of death, Thou opened the
Kingdom of Heaven to all believers.

Thou sittest at the right hand of God in the glory of the Father.
We believe that Thou wilt come to be our Judge.
We, therefore, beg Thee to help Thy servants who Thou hast
redeemed with Thy Precious Blood.
Let them be numbered with Thy saints in everlasting glory.[2]

The *Te Deum* ('To Thee, O God') is a majestic 4th century tripartite hymn of praise to God. Its first section addresses God the Father, but the second section is a most glorious expression of worship to God the Son, declaring the great themes of incarnation, atonement, resurrection and ascension. The third section does not address the Spirit, but is a series of exultant praises to God from the Psalms.

b) John Owen, English Puritan (1616-1683) from his book: *'The Person of Christ'*.[3]

'Prayer is the second general branch of divine honour - of that honour which is due and paid unto the Son, as unto the Father. This is the first exercise of divine faith - the breath of the spiritual life. ... [it is] An *ascription* of all divine properties and excellencies unto him whom we invocate [to whom we pray (ed.)] ... Hence the apostle describeth the church, or believers, and distinguisheth it, or them, from all others, by

---

[2] These verses demonstrate the point in the article though we cannot vouch for every expression of Ambrose, who wrote according to the light he had.
[3] These extracts are from the Banner of Truth magazine 1965 edn. pp.110-114.

the discharge of this duty (1 Cor. 1:2), 'With all that call on the name of our Lord Jesus Christ, both their Lord and ours.' To call on the name of the Lord Jesus expresseth solemn invocation in the way of religious worship. The Jews did call on the name of God. All others in their way called on the names of their gods. *This is that whereby the church is distinguished from them all – it calls on the name of our Lord Jesus Christ.'*

'And no motives are lacking. All that the Lord Christ hath done for us, and all the principles of love, grace, compassion, and power, from whence he hath so done did proceed are all of this [divine] nature ... Take away this duty, and the peculiar advantage of the Christian religion is destroyed. ... some will not grant that it is lawful for us to call on Christ himself. ... The Socinians grant generally that it is lawful for us to call on Christ; but they deny that it is our duty at any time so to do. But as they own that it is not our duty, so on their principles it cannot be lawful. Denying his divine person, they leave him not the proper object of prayer.'

'An instance hereof, as unto temptation, and the distress wherewith it is attended, we have in the apostle Paul. He had "a thorn in the flesh," "a messenger of Satan to buffet" him. "For this cause he besought the Lord thrice, that it might depart from him," 2 Cor. 12:7,8. He applied himself solemnly unto prayer for its removal, and that frequently. And it was the Lord – that is, the Lord Jesus Christ – unto whom he made his application. *'In the prayer to Christ, we honour the Son, even as we honour the Father.'*

c) John Nelson Darby (1800-1882) from his letters:

'Tell me I am not to worship Christ: you take away the only Christ I know. I have none other but one I do adore and worship with a thankful heart which owes all to Him. The object of John 16:27 is to give immediate confidence in the Father, in contrast with the spirit of Martha, chapter 11:22. Here the Lord says, "I say not unto you, that I will pray the Father for you: for the Father himself loveth you." Further, the question is not of worship here at all, they should ask Him nothing *(eroto)*, but were to beg *(aitero)* the Father in His name. But all the angels of God are to worship Him, every knee to bow to Him. But more: calling on the name of the Lord is, so to speak, the definition of a Christian. Paul thrice besought the Lord to take away the thorn, and the Lord heard his cry and answered. Stephen was "invoking and saying, Lord Jesus, receive my spirit." Christ is the Adonai of the Old Testament, as in Isaiah 6 and John 12 and indeed Psalm 110 and other places. The Sitter on the throne and the Lamb are associated in Revelation 5:13; indeed, it is a question if chapter 4 be not the Son in His divine Person.'

'... One who refused to worship Christ, or who did not own His mediatorship and that in every aspect, I could not walk with. But I think that worship of the Father and the worship of Christ as Mediator has a different character ...'

PRAYER TO CHRIST IN HYMNS

Many hymns express prayer, praise and worship to the blessed Son of God. The following examples will demonstrate how the hearts of hymn writers have been directed to express this attitude toward the Lord Jesus as well as to the Father.

Gathered to Thy Name, Lord Jesus,
   Losing sight of all but Thee,
Oh, what joy Thy presence gives us,
   Calling up our hearts to Thee!

Yet with reverence we would linger
   In the shadow of Thy cross,
Which has closed our hearts forever
   To the world and all its dross.

Miss C A Wellesley, 19th Century

Jesus, the very thought of Thee
   With sweetness fills the breast;
But sweeter far Thy face to see,
   And in Thy presence rest.

Bernard of Clairvaux, 12th Century

CONCLUSION

In this study on prayer and worship to the Lord Jesus, we have seen eleven examples from the New Testament demonstrating that prayer is to be directed to the blessed Son of God. There may be more. Further, we have seen examples from historical writings, and a very small sample from the many hundreds of hymns which are sung to the Lord Jesus, to demonstrate that prayer and praise (not just private, but corporate prayer and praise) is not only to be rendered to God the Father, but also to the Son. May the Lord Jesus keep us close to himself as we seek to bear corporate testimony to His lovely Name and call upon Him out of pure hearts.

PERSONAL TESTIMONY

As a new Christian, I attended one of the churches among the recognized denominations. I was taught that there was only one manner in which to pray. The Lord's Prayer[2] was dubbed a 'model prayer', and hence prayer was to be made only to God the Father in the name of His Son, the Lord Jesus Christ. Not long afterwards, I visited a meeting room where Christians gathered for prayer and Bible study. I observed that the brethren who prayed, not only addressed God as Abba, Father (see Gal. 4:6), but also prayed to the Lord Jesus. Furthermore, it was noted that the hymns and the teaching ascribed an especial dignity, affection and pre-eminence to the ascended Christ. Many years later, the Lord directed my footsteps to separate from systems where men are given pre-eminence to gather simply unto the fragrant Name of the Lord Jesus by His Spirit with them who seek to call upon Him out of a pure heart. May the blessed Lord direct all who read these few lines into greater appreciation of Himself, and obedience to His Word.

Leonard Layne

---

[2] 'Our Father, which art in heaven ...' the so-called Paternoster, is really a disciples' prayer. The 'Lord's Prayer' would be a better description of what is found in John 17!

ADDRESSING THE LORD JESUS IN PRAYER AND WORSHIP

In certain circles it has become a rare practice, and even forbidden by some, to direct worship and prayer to the Lord Jesus Christ. It has been stated that an individual in the home may address the Lord Jesus but not in the assembly; it being added that there is no one to stop someone in their home from doing so. Thus, it seems necessary to study the Scriptures as to this most important issue.

That there were those who worshipped the Lord Jesus when He was here on earth there can be no doubt. In Matthew 2 the wise men did so: they 'fell down, and worshipped Him' (verse 11), and there were many other similar incidents (See Matthew 8:2; 9:18; 14:33; 15:25; John 9:38). It might be argued, however, that this was before the cross. Then we see in Matthew 28:9, 17 and Luke 24:52 instances when there were those who worshipped the Lord Jesus after His resurrection. Indeed, in John 20 we have one of the clearest addresses to the Lord Jesus: 'Thomas answered and said unto Him, My Lord and my God' (verse 28).

Yet some may still not be convinced that it is right and proper to worship the Lord Jesus. What about now that He is ascended into heaven? Let the book of Revelation answer. In chapter 5 we read, 'The ... four and twenty elders fell down before the Lamb, ... And they sung a new song, saying, Thou art worthy to take the book, and to open the seals thereof: for Thou wast slain, and hast redeemed us to God by Thy blood, out of every kindred, and tongue, and people, and nation; And hast made us unto our God kings and priests: and we shall reign on the earth' (verses 8-10). Further, for those who insist that priesthood is for God alone, in Revelation 20:6 we read:

'They shall be priests of God and of Christ ...' If this be the proper order of service in heaven, why should it be considered inappropriate in the assembly now on earth? Are there any accounts of address to the Lord Jesus by His saints on earth after He ascended into heaven? Indeed there are.

In Acts 7 we read of Stephen, a man full of the Holy Spirit (verse 55), 'calling upon *God*, and saying, Lord Jesus, receive my spirit! And he kneeled down, and cried with a loud voice, Lord, lay not this sin to their charge' (verses 59-60). It is hard to see how a man full of the Holy Spirit would be doing something that should now be forbidden.

In Acts 9 there is a discourse between Ananias on earth and the Lord Jesus in heaven, the Lord making known His mind and a saint praying concerning it. In 2 Corinthians 12:8 the apostle Paul asked the Lord three times regarding the thorn in the flesh that was given him. Again, in 1 Timothy 1:12, he thanked Christ Jesus our Lord.

'But,' someone will say, 'These are all the prayers of individuals.' In reply, it should be observed that there are instances of companies addressing the Lord Jesus. In Acts 1 the company assembled in the upper room prayed, 'Thou, Lord, which knowest the hearts of all men, shew whether of these two Thou hast chosen' (verse 24). In Acts 13, in the church at Antioch, there were those we read of who were ministering to the Lord (verse 2). It is companies that the apostle exhorts to speak 'to yourselves in psalms and hymns and spiritual songs, singing and making melody in your heart to the Lord' (Eph. 5:19. See also Col. 3:16).

It must be emphasised that in all these references to the Lord, it is the Lord Jesus who is directly addressed and not the Father. Indeed, it is doubtful if we are correct in addressing the Father as Lord, since, 'to us there is but one God, the Father, ... and one Lord Jesus Christ' (1 Cor. 8:6). Such a mode of address seems to be based on the usage of LORD in the Old Testament (in the King James Translation), before the Father was revealed in the Person of the Son.

We are all learners in the matter of prayer (Luke 11:1) and I do not desire to be critical. But is it not the case that one of the characteristics of Christianity is being assailed in the attempt to forbid prayer and worship to the Lord Jesus? It would seem from the book of Acts that calling on the Lord's Name was the hallmark of a Christian. In chapter 9 Ananias, in his prayer to the Lord, speaks of Saul of Tarsus as having 'authority from the chief priests to bind all that call on Thy Name' (verse 14). And again, in verse 21, some were asking, 'Is not this he that destroyed them which called on this Name in Jerusalem ...?' Indeed, is one saved who has not called on the Name of the Lord? (See Acts 2:21 and Rom. 10:13). How are we to be saved if we are not to call on the Lord's Name? From 1 Corinthians 1:2 it would appear to be the normal thing for Christians to address the Lord Jesus: 'Unto the church of God which is at Corinth, ... with all that in every place call upon the Name of Jesus Christ our Lord.' Or, now that things are abnormal: 'with them that call on the Lord out of a pure heart' (2 Tim. 2:22). Whereas to be saved the call need only be once made, the references to calling on the Lord's Name by the Christian company are in the continuous tense and would suggest that saints would normally be calling on the Lord. As to calling on the Name of the Lord, it would seem abundantly clear from Scripture that it conveys, among other things, the idea of:

- a recognition of His deity and power (See 1 Kings 18:24; 2 Kings 5:11);
- a submission to His authority and acknowledgement of His rights (Jer. 10:25);
- A call to Him for help in the expectation of an answer (1 Kings 18; 2 Kings 5; Psa. 99:6; Zech. 13:9);
- an approach to Him in worship and thanksgiving (Psa. 116:17).

It would be associated with the place where He dwells (see Jer. 3:17). Once this was at Jerusalem, as it will be again in the future, but today we know the system of grace which comes from 'Jerusalem ... above' (Gal. 4:26). Thus we gather to the Lord's Name, to act for the Lord in His absence, to invite His presence, to offer Him our praise and worship as we break bread in remembrance of Him, and to seek His mind and blessing.

It must be stressed that this does not rule out prayer and worship to God the Father. The matter for prayer should decide the Person to be addressed. For example, the Lord Jesus gave the commission to preach the gospel and thus, as the Lord's servant, I would seek direction from Him about this. It is God who desires that all men should be saved and hence our pleadings for the lost may be addressed to God (1 Tim. 2:3-4). And as children of God, we can address the Father.

With regard to the Lord's supper, it is only fitting to address the Lord Jesus, for we break bread in remembrance of Him. It is the church's affectionate response to Christ who has loved and given Himself for her. As the Lord in the midst leads the praise of His own to the Father (Heb. 2:12), God is worshipped according to the way He has made Himself known in the Person of His Son (John 4:23-24).

It is interesting that the whole canon of Scripture concludes with a prayer to the Lord: 'Even so, come, Lord Jesus' (Rev. 22:20). Well may every believer pray such a prayer daily and mean it. But is it not that the Lord Jesus, in a final appeal to His own here in this world, desires bridal affections in the assembly; that His own may be yearning for His actual presence as much as He desires to have them with Him? 'The Spirit and the bride say, Come' (Rev. 22:17).

Mark Best

Other titles in the Fountain Series:

1. *Daniel's Seventy Weeks*
   by William Kelly
2. *Thou and Thy House, or the Christian at Home*
   by C H Mackintosh
3. *Kings and Priests*
   by William Kelly
4. *The All-sufficiency of the Name of Jesus*
   by C H Mackintosh
5. *The Church of the Living God, the House of God and The Body of Christ*
   by W J Lowe
6. *A Child of Wisdom*
   by Henrik Gautesen
7. *Unity: what is it? and am I confessing it?*
   by C H Mackintosh
8. *The Christian Woman*
   by A J Pollock
9. *The Old Nature and the New Birth; or the New Convert and his difficulties*
   by Geo Cutting
10. *Mephibosheth, Lame of Both his Feet, or, the Kindness of God*
    by Charles Stanley
11. *My Awakening, my Quickening, my Sealing and my Deliverance*
    by Richard Holden
12. *To Whom do you Pray?*
    by Leonard Layne and Mark Best
13. *The Rise of Clericalism in Early Christianity*
    by Gerard H Kramer

Ask for our free catalogue, available from the publisher's office.

Chapter Two
Fountain House, Conduit Mews, London SE18 7AP
www.chaptertwobooks.org.uk, e-mail chapter2uk@aol.com